Spirit's Spark

Stories and Musings in Poems

Milly White

Published by
HenschelHAUS Publishing, Inc.
Milwaukee, WI
www.henschelHAUSbooks.com

ISBN: 978159598-701-3
E-ISBN: 978159598-721-1
Library of Congress Control Number: 2019930378

Cover photo by Milly White, "Falmouth Sunset"
Author photo, title page, by Karen Ruggiero

Contents

Introduction

As our transformations go on, sometimes so slowly
that we weep with despair,
know that we have mystical messengers
surrounding us, sometimes unaware,
to remind us of our immortality
and strength and knowing.

So, on May 28th, 2018, 8:53 am, the above "message poem" flashed into my head whilst I was e-mailing a friend, telling her about a dear little nephew of ours. I had sent a picture to her of his kissing my cheek, and I told her that he was deeply loved and Spirit has been with him. Now you may ask: "What's with the exact time and date bit? Well, using a computer, and that computer keeping track of things for me, has allowed my looking back at this amazing time of being "gifted" with poems that "come to me". Yes, many times I read them and say: "Yikes, did I write that?"

Now, I should back up a bit, and tell you that I had written some poetry about 30 years ago, just for myself, and then a few for friends. I included a revised few in this book. Some had just "come" to me, but certainly not with the force that they have changed my life around, since late 2017 to the present.

Another thing that you might want to know is that I had never heard about certain poets, no less read their poems, including Mary Oliver, Hafiz, Rabindranath Tagore, and Rainer Maria Rilke, to mention my favorites. I had been writing poems for a while from late December 2017 before people gifted me with their books or I learned of their names.

With no offense meant, I just did not read poetry. When I finally did hear about them and was given or bought their books, I was amazed at their writing. I felt a close connection that I've never, ever felt before when reading poetry. I get chills and understand on such a deep level what they are expressing, and how it makes me feel.

In addition, I had never heard the word, "awakening," until I was given a book about such things very recently. I'd read Oliver Sacks' *Musicophilia*, which gave me some clues about what was going on.

You may notice, as you go along, that many of the poems have more than a bit of a relationship with one or more of the others. They each tell a true story and/or poetic interpretation of how or why they "came" to me.

If you would like to share your own stories, my e-mail address is:
whitemilly31@gmail.com

Acknowledgments

I want to thank people who have helped me during the writing and publishing of "Spirit's Spark," and who, (despite my kicking and protesting with, "Oh, no, I won't publish!") kept up with suggestions and encouragement anyway.

Terri Arthur, author extraordinaire, who appears in a poem within, made my life 5 zillion times easier by preparing, then teaching ME how to put the poems within Word, (I always write them and edit them by hand, first). She showed me how to add pictures, then how to create the whole book of poems in some magical Word process.

This was sent in icons to Kira Henschel, Terri's publisher. (Kira had said "yes," when I asked her if she would publish "Spirit's Spark" for me. Brave woman!!!)

Another thing about Terri; when she thought some poems needed more editing or re-writing or new placing in the book, she told me so and why. Interestingly, I had had the same feeling about those very poems, too. I am grateful for her insight and having never lost her patience with my "techie" ignorance and my lack of patience with myself. Many, many thanks, Terri.

From the beginning (December 2017), Karen Ruggiero, my friend, had been keeping track of the poems by putting them in a file each time I'd send them over for her to read via e-mail. Much later, I found out that the "file" was IN her computer. Uh, I had thought she meant in a file cabinet. When she said they should be published in a book, I said, "Yikes, no." I think her next remark was: "If YOU don't, I WILL, because they should be published; and I've got them ALL in a file, so I can." (I'm still picturing a file cabinet). I think when she said I was a "poet," that's when it started to sink in. Yikes!

I thank Karen for her patience, her unique critiques, and her caring enough to gently push me toward publishing, sometimes calling me "Mildred." This made me pay attention, (she knew it would) and also made me laugh. How could I refuse, especially when she'd raise one eyebrow as she said: "Mildred"? Moreover, Karen took the author photo on the title page when we were at dinner before a "Friends of Cape Wildlife" presentation, as well as other photos throughout the book. Thank you so very much, Karen.

Now I want to tell you about our writers' group. It was conceived by Jean Nadzeika, our illustrious leader. Many of us had attended a monthly reading project at Waquoit Congregational Church's Parish Hall. Jean had chosen a book of essays called, *This I Believe*. We would read the book, choose, and then read our favorite essays to the group, and perhaps write our own. By then, several of us wanted to continue together beyond the allotted time. Bless her heart, Jean was delighted.

The larger group became a smaller group, with our choosing a name, "Word Weavers."

It was adopted from a diverse, but welcoming writers' group in a small southern mountain town where Jean had settled for a while. We added "Waquoit" and Waquoit Word Weavers was born.

As time went by, our members became close friends, who felt a dedication to each other's thoughts and writings, and even art work, as much as to our own. We are Jean Nadzeika, Bobbi Keane, Jackie Finney, Betty Flagg, Sally Gasperoni, and yours truly. Several others, like Jane Tanner, Christine Laughead, and Beth Rockwell are recent arrivals, and a few others come and go as time or work allow.

I'm not speaking for just myself when I say that we look forward to each meeting with great anticipation. It goes beyond the writing or art we hear or see; it goes to the heart of each person's feelings, the joy in seeing such creations develop. Can you tell, dear reader, how grateful I am for each of them?

Now, speaking of encouragement brings me to Jan Smith-Rushton. A retired Methodist minister, Jan had asked me if she could interview me for a course she was taking. To make a long story short, her questions about spirituality took me back to my childhood and back again. Months later, as the poems started "coming in," this spiritual life review by Jan really helped me understand some of what was going on. When I first showed her my poems, wow, like Terri and Karen, and the Waquoit Word Weavers, Jan seemed excited about them and for me. She helped me with the title, as well. Later, when I told her that Kira had said "Yes" to publishing the book, she clapped her hands in delight. Her hubby, Bob, a gentle man with a great sense of humor, quietly said: "Uh, oh, two authors in one household!!!!"

I especially want to thank my daughter, Bonnie White, and my granddaughter, Cassidy White-Macfarlane. They have been so very supportive, with Cassidy requesting that I write a poem to which she could write music, which she has. "Re-tuned Heart" is in memory of my sister, Jan Butler, who died 6/27/16. Four poems about Bonnie's babyhood and early childhood are also in the book. She graciously allowed me to include them. Thank you, Bonnie. I am so grateful to have you in my life.

I'm not sure that this book would exist if Bonnie had not encouraged my getting more involved in on-line computer activities. Once again, my "kicking and screaming" were overcome by her reasoned and gentle persuasion. Hence, her childhood home, Grasmere, was enshrined for a while within a FaceBook tribute a number of years ago. Grasmere's revised poem is included herein, along with some accompanying pictures from the mid-1900s.

Will Felder inspired "Seal" with his very exciting and true story, just told from Seal's point of view. "Spark of Creativity" is Fran Rivera's doing.

Amy Tufts, a new friend, got "Mother to Mother" going, when I thought the book was finished, but, "Oh, no," back to my writing pad. She reminded me of an amazing episode I had told her about years ago; and yes, you guessed it, a poem "popped" in and was born.

I mention Denise Tornick and send her many thanks as well. Denise is my mentor about cats and other creatures and has been my very good friend since the Grasmere days.

If I have left some people out, please forgive my "fuzzy" brain. So many folks "started" the poems by saying something that then "sparked" ideas. Some may not even realize they did. When that happened, zingo, into my brain then into a poem. Of course, Nell Fields' sermons could have had me writing for years to come, and maybe will. Look for "grasp the golden threads" as one example.

And on and on...

Love, Milly

Victoria Falls (photo by M. White)

Gift of a Rainbow

As dawn's rays of sunlight
filter through the new leaves of spring
and dapple my curtains,
I think of you.

The days now have color; no more the gray monotones
that posted themselves like sentries
along my path,
forbidding glimpses of joy.

What miracle brought you into my life?
Like a beacon of light, you shine
into the corners of my soul,
reflecting through and illuminating
each moment of the day.

At last, at night, resisting sleep, I hold you in my heart
and drift along on sunlit waters with my dreams
and you.

(1986)

Photo by M. White

Grasmere Revisited (Photo by Ruth Wilnor White)

Grasmere Revisited

So, at times unsure, I feel a lump form
in my throat.
Grasmere's been my home,
my way of life for years.
I've written poems to her.
Though built of stones, circled with trees
and lakes and hills,
she hears my words of love.
She is alive, and I can hear her whisper in the night:
"Will you come back to me again?"
Whilst daily work distracts my mind from memories
that wait to overthrow the plans
for love anew,
whose silken webs surround my healing heart
and pull me toward the coast;
It matters not, for Grasmere claims, and
interrupts with whispering to me:
"Will you come back to me again?"
The boulders mock me, "We've been here since
glacial forces pushed us south
and scattered us like pebbles
in the waves at sea;
WE cannot leave, our children form her very core."
Again I hear their whispers in my dreams:
"Will you come back to us again?"
Now but a vestige of his former self, the mighty Oak
recalls the swing upon his limb from which
a girl and collie dog did fly.
Still standing guard behind the gated entrance there,
he also asks, in quiet dignity, the same refrain
that haunts my sleep each night.
I hear their calls,
my soul is stretched between the valleys, hills and ponds
and ocean, sand and sky.

The choice is mine, and so I choose to follow love,
to follow roads out to its source, where forests
meet the sea.
So, I must answer them with surety of heart's desire,
I answer them, with trembling voice
"I will come back and visit you again."

Photo by Karen Ruggiero

Christmas Morning

She welcomed me into the place of healing,
the angel volunteer, with the name of a flower.
I thanked her for being here on Christmas morning.
"We are here, so others can celebrate on their Holy Day",
said this daughter of Sarah and Naomi and Ruth.

My charioteer, her spouse, parted the way to the inner rooms,
where the angels of healing took care of me
as if I were their own.

"Fear not", and I didn't.
"You are not alone", and I never was.

So, as from the entry way, escorted by the children of David
to the inner core, where I was cared for
by the children of many faiths and from many lands,
we were as One Spirit
as close as a prayer
as close as a song
as close as a heartbeat.

Falmouth sunset (Photo by M. White)

The Invitation

So she said, "Yayyy, see you for lunch!"
Then followed some of the sweetest words I'd heard
that day, or in a week:
"Come earlier 'cuz I'll be baking and
you can pick out the crumbs!!"
Oh, my former life flashed and tumbled in my brain.
I heard my sister, (with a laugh), chiding me
for doing such a thing. (For I had)
And yet, and YET, years into this present life,
could this be real? I was invited,
INVITED to gather crumbs
fallen from the cake, and
then was promised more to come!
Well, how could this be? It was a dream,
it was a fantasy come true !
Go ahead, go ahead--
some of you may laugh;
but others won't,
(you know who you are).
One last thing that tingled my brain again,
that tingled my tongue even more was the news,
THE NEWS
It was a Blue Ribbon winning Butter Crumb Cake
I was invited to pick crumbs from,
(and many will share delight
in my luck).
For is it not incredible, is it not amazing how much joy,
how much happiness can be received,
can be given in simple words,
in simple gifts,
in simple invitations?

"I'll be baking, and you can pick out the crumbs."

Spirit's Spark

Photo by Jan Butler

Jan in Winter

As my sister used to say, on a colder than cold day,

"I think my eyeballs are freezing."

I thought that was a funny thing to say

and certainly something I would not want to feel.

But I went out to feed the critters on a morning

when it was colder than cold.

So, Jan came to me, and said, "Now you know what I meant."

And I did, and I laughed and cried all at the same time.

Photo by M. White

Sunrise (Photo by M. White)

Remembering

Strange perhaps, a poem about poems,
for when they flood my brain,
I need to sort the thoughts,
before they vanish in the clouds.

I need to write at least a word
or a name or a beginning line,
when a word or a name or
a beginning line seem as requests
from afar,

until the writing's done and mulling thoughts
are stilled by Spirit's gentling voice,
which tells me: "Read this poem
to find the next."

Montrose sunset (Photo by M. White)

Sir Davis (Photo by M. White)

Sir Davis

Five plus years ago, thru our deck door

his emerald eyes stared coolly into mine.

"Who sent you?" (I fully knowing who it was,

his look-a-like, who'd "passed away" two years before,

but had never really left).

Still he sat, he did not blink those calm and knowing eyes,

waiting for the lunch foretold by Pearl-a-kins the Fair.

She'd told him of a safer life, where he could come and go

through secret fencing holes his size that would keep coyotes out.

Coming to a greater age, he knew he must retire

from begging food
and catching less
and finding caves in snow.

So, there he was, that August day, all matted hair and wounded ear

and searched my soul with emerald eyes,

to stake his claim and make our house his home.

Sir Davis (Photos by M. White)

MV—Photo by M. White

Was it You?

Whilst I was preparing my meal for later in the day,
was your mantra calling?
For this poem pushed in homemade biscuits
as its title, or perhaps its beginning words.
I wrote the first draft in pencil, so that as they flooded in
I could erase and write and correct and write,
with less interruption.
I am hearing:
"The Sermon on the Mount is about so much more than food."
What am I really hearing as it flows into my mind?

This then I know, my Friend, when you present to me
a veggie meal,
or spontaneous, "mantra-driven biscuits."
As I receive them, my heart fills with another
kind of nourishment.
It understands as it receives,
because it's food for the soul from you.

Spirit's Spark

Photo by Karen Ruggiero

Knowing

When I had wept tears of grief at other times,
Of course I understood.

But when tears of joy rained thru my soul
I could NOT understand.

This was new, this joyful weeping,
And as its meaning came slowly,
I marveled at the recognition
of new beginnings.

Feeling Spirit's love within me, I quieted my very being
with the mystic celebration of the prayer cycle of song,
the prayer cycle of love,
and rejoiced.

Both elephant photos by Gina Keller

Mother to Mother

The giant gray shapes emerged
from between the thorn trees
where they had been feeding
unseen.
The young teenagers flapped their large ears,
bellowed and charged our jeep to impress
the others,
including the tiniest who ran beneath
their mothers' bellies looking for comfort and food.
A lady with our group quietly exclaimed
with trembling voice
that the herd was closing ranks behind us.
Our driver guide spoke in low and reassuring tones,
as we were slowly surrounded by the herd.

Oh my, the Matriarch, six feet away,
rumbling low and gentle things,
quieted her family, who swayed and blew dust
and gathered babies to their sides.
Fascinated, but somehow not afraid,
I remembered Denise's lessons of talking to cats,
starting with really slow eye blinks
then picturing----well, for a cat---salmon in his dish.

Surely, an elephant, a lovely Matriarch,
would appreciate slowly blinking eyes
and pictures sent of tasty leaves and wild squash.
Thus, catching her eyes and sending
those thoughts, with love, her way,
slowly blinking and sending tasty pictures,
I continued,
until at last, she blinked as well.
Later after our exchanges, this great, gray Matriarch turned
and took her family back the way they'd come.
One last look my way, Mother to Mother, an understanding
that will last a lifetime.

Spirit's Spark

Photo by Bonnie White

Harmonious Connections

When each idea or feeling commands
my attention, and it's all that I can hear,
and about all that I can think;
I am led, or directed toward the way
that makes me look deeper,
or perhaps beyond,
to fathom why the "message" left its spiral place
to be heard, to be known,
to be understood.
I've been asked what thing, or strange events cause
the avalanche or symphony
within my being, within my soul to bring
these thoughts to light.
I cannot say, except that gems of knowing
have been there waiting,
waiting for their dormancy to end,
the ancient memories or cosmic truths to awaken me
and come here for me to share;
their urgency apparent, as I must write.
This I know, when I listen to the songs they bring,
they settle, I settle, as I work their words around.
Until with Spirit's presence like a gentle touch,
a mother's touch, surrounding me with Love,
I can then rest, my work is done, and I proclaim:
"They're safely in a poem, at last."

Both Sir Davis photos by Milly White

Sir Davis Revisited

So, every night, I say a word or two of love,
as he rolls on the bed, from one side to the other.
The pink of his nose blends into the pink and white of his lips,
and somehow, he creates a smile that enchants the heart.
In his deepest sleep, sometimes he reaches out his paw to me,
an invitation to begin my nightly time of praise.

You see, it's been five plus years since he came here,
ragged, hungry, yet imperious,
so sure of himself, he took my breath away.
He'd spent at least a decade out in weather fair or foul,
with hidey-holes for shelter, scrounging food each place he'd go,
until at last he heard the message only he
could understand, and he'd found himself this home.
Now in times of slumber, deep within his feline dreams, he's still alert,
for as I say my words of praise, he hears and starts to purr.

His favorite time's when Spring has hatched the tiny buds of Oak,
and gentle beams of light warm places just for him.
Up on the deck, he stretches his great length of self
all white and black, in greetings to the Sun.
Unrestrained by thoughts of doom or coming winter cold,
his dreams are kinder now, echoing the praise and love
he heard the nights before.

He learned that he could trust us, he could tell us with his eyes.
Closed doors that once would panic him, we'd open
when he stared.
What most he cherished was his freedom
that forever would remain,
but wandering off for distances became a thing no more.

So, in this house of learning, we found that this was true;
Love can be a living force in everyone,
a grant of Grace for all.

Newgrange, Ireland, circa 3200 BC (photo by M. White)

The Spiral

The messages within the messages spiral outward.
They come to you in random words, or songs that are
the Music of the Spheres.
When in songs, they may remain with you all day,
or comfort you at night,
when you cannot sleep before the dawn.

Before the start of day unravels their meanings
as they arc thru time and perhaps faster than the speed of light;
as they unwind like a ball of string or expand with the Milky Way,
prepare yourself.
Prepare yourself to grasp the golden threads,
the golden promises given, when you were but a child.

Grasp them as your day begins, with singing or dancing or praising,
holding close those remembrances from so long ago,
from beyond the stars.
Reclaim those Truths, the Knowing who you are,
cloaked in Strength and Courage,
Joy and Love
to start your life, each day, anew.

Spirit's Spark

Photo by Jan Butler

Spark of Creativity

There is a lady in the lab who always greets me by my name,
before I even sign in.
This happens, no matter how busy they are,
or how long it's been between visits.
How can she do that? How does she maintain
that calm, that kindness,
and always remember my name?
(Somehow, I suspect, it is the same for every patient she sees.)
Still, I marvel, and feel special, and each lab time
I hope for enough time to talk,
at least, "How have you been?", "How were your holidays?"
(You know, the usual).
This time she listened closely to my Christmas Day story,
my "shocking" Christmas Day tale,
when rhythm was restored to my heart.
But even more important, I shared the wonder,
the wonder of the poems that now pop into my brain,
carried on a song, or a name, or a random phrase.
So, having heard my story, without blinking her eyes,
without a thought or doubt,
she plucked a phrase from spiraling stars
where poems are born, and sent it to my soul;
For then she said:
"Just like a spark of creativity"
"Oh," I gasped; her words were like a bolt of lightning, a pulse
of recognition
that made my face and eyes light up, (she later said.)
For I'd been gifted by this Angel in the lab
on just an ordinary day,
not on Christmas, like before,
not in the Church, two times before,
or late at night when whispering a prayer.
Now, as these waves of Knowing flooded my Soul,
in this place of healing, in this place of kindness,
I'd been gifted once again, to understand how poems arrive
as Harmonious Connections,
and now, perhaps, the why.

Not Even Close

"I'm glad you like it", she said, when I became effusive
over her Valentine gift for me.
Pictures of owls were on the front cover
and had made me smile.

But as my eyes had drifted to the author's name, I gasped,
drew in that tell-tale breath that spoke volumes
about the great delight in my heart.
"Mary Oliver", I cried out. " Where did you find this?"
(which really was besides the point)

For despite her busy, busy days, she'd taken time
to follow through to find the perfect gift for me,
a gift of love.

"I'm glad you like it," she said again. Said I to her,
"Dear One, not even close."

Lotus

Four Crows and the Chant

Shining in the sun, his black feathers astir from agitation,
he looked back and forth,
cawing, calling to his friends in distant trees.
At last, one by one they joined him on the great Oak's branch,
as I with thanks, sighed the chant aloud;
the simple sounding chant that echoes down thru Buddhist past;
the peaceful law each living thing can know.
Coyote, Squirrel, or Butterfly,
the giant Oak, or Grasses swaying near the sea,
can feel it's mystic waves.
To witness this, just after dawn, or evening's call,
I've watched one Squirrel sit up and HEAR, as others scampered by;
or Chickadee join in with song as part of HIS refrain.

Back to the Crows, I wondered which of them
would turn to hear the chant and which of them would leave.
At first, with no attention paid, they readied for their flight,
until the chant was multiplied at least a dozen times.

Now picture this, within your mind, within your soul
where Spirit lives.
Each Crow slowly turned in line to face me,
as mystic chanting rose toward great Oak's branch.
Each Crow bowed, as if in response to prayer,
then lifted up on shining wings together,
spiraling out and far beyond the trees.
Then they flew into the sky above me, calling back,
perhaps announcing things
that only they knew, THEY knew, before the chant.

Spirit's Spark

Shims and other Cedar Shingle Musings

The fragrance compelled my nose to follow it,
around the side, and to the back,
where a giant dumpster stood.
Oh, old Cedar shingles,
you're all that's left of your soft bark trunks
with cores of lovely red,
and the aroma that takes me back
to shady nooks,
in forests that I loved to roam.

But memories are not all that you will know,
for your uses NOW are myriad;
a few of us have named them one by one
and even two.
Bob wanted you for shims, and Jan remembered scenes
or birds painted on your golden sides as crafts.
But perhaps you'd enjoy helping a gardener
who'd place your sharp edge down into the earth
from where you were born,
to keep the earthworms tucked into the garden,
whilst you keep the chewers
of the tiny veggie rootlets out.

So, worry not, we won't forget you;
as we know a lovely song about you.
For before you covered and protected Parish Hall,
you and others like you lived in
Green Cathedrals of our Scouting days.
We knew YOU as a "priestly cedar sighing",
in a " hallowed forest shrine".
And so we always will.

Provincetown dunes (Photo by M. White)

Seal

(Inspired by Will Felder)

His brindled brown and gray head raised as he caught
the slightest change in scents.
Wind had lifted once again along the coast;
the colony prepared for hunting,
but waited for a sign.
As soft dark eyes searched, his whiskers trembled
with each exploring of the air.
It was not the smell of large machines that raced along
to scatter or to even harm his herd;
and yet he waited.
Ah, he remembered now, the time "they" came before,
and Great Whites headed out to sea when
the sharks saw the "others" here.
The scent grew stronger; then there "they" were--
a single "flipper" joining each
pair of legs;
Their fragile bodies each tethered to the sky
by a cord to a single flying, billowing wing.
So, Seal barked commands: "We will join together;
we will stay the course beyond the sharks",
as their sun kissed, dappled bodies
slipped into the water
off the beach.
And so it came to pass, these two groups joined again as one,
One to swim and hunt in safety;
the other to fly,
To fly with joy, to fly with pure abandon
upon the tops of waves,
on top of waves in sunlit seas, drawn along by kites
that billowed, and were tethered to the wind.

~ 35 ~

Harbinger of Spring, April 7, 1968

You "announced" your plans for Monday, on a Sunday,
on a working-in-the-garden day, when daffodils
and tulips bloomed.
For later, after dinner, I (laughing) said to Peg, " I'm fine,
just a little back-ache, too much bending, too much raking",
as they left for home that night.
I should have known, this child of ours, this child called "Chip"
(until we'd had the chance to meet),
just could not wait.
As buds on trees can't stop their leaves from opening,
nor bulbs stay dormant in the warming ground,
you could not stop your Soul's awakening;
it must be soon, so much to do.
As returning wood thrush sang their haunting love calls,
as peepers trilled their nightly call,
you hunkered down to start your new adventure
from warmth of mother's nest
to unfamiliar light and cold.
Down we went on stony roads in growing darkness,
round chilling curves on Skylands roads.
Of course this bumpy trip just helped to hasten
the meeting of, the long awaited meeting of,
our child, our precious harbinger of Spring.

Clara Karl ("Gooma") and Bonnie (Photo by M. White

Day You Were Born, April 8, 1968

When they brought you to us, lovely child of Spring,
I stared as your eyes reflected back to mine.
Your tiny Dutch Grandma's face
looked up at me,
and I looked back in wonder.
I hope you felt my love and saw the love
in your father's eyes, so much like yours,
sparkling with delight.

Then Gooma joined us from the chapel down the hall,
where she had sung with other folks.
They mourned for King whose dying, days before,
had torn apart our land and hearts.
Alerted once again to changes coming, my soul cried out.
Please understand: Born in this time of war,
but living with the dreams of peace,
might be your destiny.
Born in this time of racial despair, marching
and protesting all violence,
but with the dreams of new beginnings,
whom to follow?

Yet with a sigh, (that changed in years to: "Oh, Mom"),
you nestled in and drifted off to sleep,
to wander through your own dreams,
perhaps to hear the voices from a far off time,
whispering lessons from a far off place
beyond the stars.

So, once again you sighed, as I held your tiny hand
in a caress.

Grasmere side gate (Photo by Bonnie White)

Bonnie's First Day Home, April 12, 1968

This first day home with you plays like a video in my mind.
When I tell of the preparations we took
to try to make things work out,
you may laugh, as I did remembering.
For after we unlocked the Skylands Gate, festooned with signs
that Annie made, welcoming you home—I began to worry anew.
Halfway up the two mile drive, I said to John,
"I've got it, YOU carry her in and I will greet Timmy,"
(who had pulled out an electric plug
and chewed it in frustration the night before).
So with that plan, with quaking hearts, we proceeded.
Grasmere Gatehouse awaited you, whilst Tim awaited me.
Well, it worked!! He danced, he rolled over,
he danced again, waving front paws in the air.
Never before had this small, black, fuzzy poodle displayed
such joy, such excitement, as I scooped him up.
Later, I sat in the rocker—Timmy sat on the couch.
You were put in my arms, my sweet, dear daughter love,
you were home at last, our family complete!
Tim slowly sidled over on the couch, reached out his paw,
and looked at us.
"This is your sister, Tim, her name is Bonnie,"
as I held you up, so that he could see.
He moved gently forward, took one inquisitive look
and one discerning sniff,
then another long inquiring snuffle,
and in a flash, as fast as he could pivot,
as only Balanchine could do,
he raced away, sat down,
with his curly back toward us,
perhaps never to return again.

At least not for a long, long time.

Bonnie & Tim
(Photo by M. White)

Bonnie and John. Both photos are reproduced from an old 8mm-film (M. White)

Future Vistas

Springtime born, the little girl with "rabbit ears" upon her hat,
was running through a field of flowers,
followed by a handsome lad, three months her senior,
racing to keep up.
When he did at last, with gentle touch, he took her arm
and turned her to his kiss.
At first, she welcomed sweet, soft lips upon her velvet cheek,
once, twice, and yet once more.
But in a flash she spun around through flowers
toward the wide, long vista,
going her own way, on tiny feet, coursing along
as if to lift off and fly.
Her father called out for her return; but on she flew,
her "bunny ears" kept cadence with her feet.
And even as her dad caught up, he smiled, encouraging
her determined run, as I recorded every step,
every step that took her far from me.
For on this loveliest of days, I knew somehow, her life
was being planned and practiced by herself,
in measured steps, in faster starts.
Preparing for her own life's Vistas, filled with myriad
adventures—all around the world she'd go.
A woman who could make her way alone at times,
and glory in the run.

Terri Arthur and postcard book (Photo by M. White)

Ladies of the Lamp

She'd been a caregiver all her life, as big sister,
then teacher, nurse, and leader;
a woman to whom all could turn
for advice and help.
So, on the "dark and stormy night," her life re-focused;
the night that sent her mind and her heart
and her soul on adventures afar
and thousands of miles to distant lands.
This first night of the journey may be hard to believe,
(but I was witness to the truth); the night when only fire
in the hearth, and candles on the mantel
gave her warmth and light.

A birthday book she'd left alone for months, but was easiest
to read by flickering flames, caught little interest.
Until mid-book, MID-BOOK, she came upon the page where all
distraction ceased.
Macabre postcards a century old, (with tales of what they meant)
made her look at them once more, and again,
with her promise that come morning, she'd learn
about this nurse.
Never had she heard her name before this night.
But THEY would know, the nurse historians,
the experts, the committees from the archives,
they would know, tomorrow.
So, cozy by the fire, orange cat nestled in her lap,
storm blowing snow and ice
against the window panes,
she drifted away
with questions circling her mind *(continued)*

Edith Cavell, World War I Nurse (public domain image)

Ladies of the Lamp *(continued)*

And in that time, began adventures of a nameless kind,
for out of storm and candlelight
came whispered stories
AND a plea;
"Oh, Sister of the Lamp, bring my voice alive again.
It is only through compassion and love
that the world will change,
not through war."
As Terri awakened to a furnace humming, awakened to
a clear blue sky,
it seemed the quiet voice the night before
had come from distant dreams, a distant time.
And yet, and YET, she felt possessed
by KNOWING she must follow through.
Perhaps it was a week or more before she learned the truth.
Of experts called, none recognized the noble nurse;
though some had heard their mothers speak her name
in reverential tones.
So, not to be stopped, nor have her fervent search delayed,
our modern "Lady of the Lamp"
forged on, until she found her Hero,
to resurrect her life.
OR perhaps, as some suspect, and many know, (as I a witness do)
that Edith Cavell found our Terri, whose writings
shed eternal light, whose writings filled the void,
allowing Edith's voice to echo,
beyond the ages, beyond the stars
for many years to come.

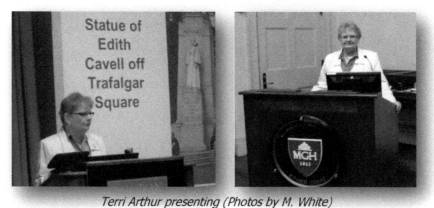

Terri Arthur presenting (Photos by M. White)

Sir Davis (Photo by M. White)

Conversations With a Blue-Winged Warbler

Watch how he "flits" his feathers as he moves from finch food
to the suet.
Hear his "bzzzt" as he waits impatiently
for the food lady
to finish her rounds.
He arrived mid April, and that first day,
he almost sat on my head,
bzzzing that funny song, which I tried to bzzzt back.
'Twas too hard for me to do, but he was gracious
or so hungry that he stayed to eat.
Lovely little bird, smaller than a goldfinch,
but watch him make the others move,
(except the Blue Jay).
Today, I told him how beautiful he was,
as he bzzzt and flitted in the trees;
and how I loved his presence
at our home.
Then, Sir Davis came behind me, through deck sliders.
See how grand and courtly is this long-haired cat?
Actually, imperial, the black butterfly "crown"
upon his head.
His look says: "I am the one you talk to, praise and
call me "handsome guy".
He asks:
"Why are you talking now, into the air it seems,
when I have been inside?"
So, Blue-Wing bzzzt, and Davis stared, a stalemate sure to end.
This way it did, as Davis walked sedately down the stairs,
whilst Blue-Wing bzzzt and flitted
and ate again once more.

Black squirrel (Photo by M. White)

Spirit in the Morning

In the quiet of the early morning,
I feel Spirit's presence closer
than at other times.

Wondering why, perhaps as only Libras do,
I think that Spirit's smaller creatures
are awakening then and starting
their new day in praise.

This pure echo of the love of Spirit rises
as the Sun does,
and in the music of the birds.

And so, together we can glory in that knowing
and in gratefulness as One.

Chickadee and cardinals (Photo by M. White)
Crows on opposite page (Photos by M. White)

Morning with the Crows

Oh, you cheeky Crows, listen to your noisy cawing.
I guess you don't remember, but should know
I do have more to do before you get your treats,
and they ARE just TREATS.
For I know you eat your meals all day finding berries in the woods,
and shellfish washed upon the shore,
and on Thursdays, salvaged garbage is the lunch du jour.
But you don't realize that I tempt you here with treats to hear you talk
and teach your children, who are following your lead.
So, you kings and queens of sky and wind, you too
were downy chicks, all heads with beaks that opened wide
when your parents brought you food.

Your chicks have glossy feathers now that reflect light from the sun
and hypnotize me as you all lift off in most glorious flight.
Yet you caw, seemingly unaware that I must sweep the deck,
and put out seeds and corn for the smaller ones who wait their turns,
like Cardinals, Chipmunks and Chickadees.
And don't forget the pesky Squirrels who'd love to grab your treats.
There are your crested cousins, Jays, who told you that I'm here at last,
but, ah, they are unafraid, grabbing corn AND treats and taking off,
their iridescent blue and white vanishing up to great Oak's limbs.

Sometimes you sit above and wait and preen your handsome selves
and send to me a feather light and free, a gift it seems.
It floats along on waves of wind, gently rocking as a tiny boat
that settles when I reach out and it nestles in my hand.
Thanking you, my Corvid friends, I spread your treats and slowly back away
in wonderment and joy, as one by one you clear the gate in silence,
lightly land inside, and eat.

In the Best of Times

I am Eagle
in the best of times.

Without the gift of flight,
I still can soar
and witness love
and Spirit's attempts
to bring forward in each of us
the hidden treasures
of joy and grace
and forgiveness.

It can happen in a heartbeat
or in finding a friend who knows
your soul.

Skylands vista (Photo by Ruth Wilnor White)

Transformation of Grief

Like some gray cloud, it slips upon you unprepared.
Though pushed around a corner on a brighter day,
it sits there waiting for a verse
or song that turns your mind to vistas laced with sunshine
that you once had shared.
It waits for empty moments in the day, not filled with purpose to delay
its re-emerging once again,
to cloak your heart with its cold weight,
and neither light nor sound will penetrate its dreary shape.

Ah, will it disappear some day, or be transformed to fibers
of a lighter gauge?
Though resting on your thoughts of them, whose passing
left behind that shroud of gray,
it will not cause such pain nor blindness to a joyous scene.

As when birds fly back to nest in woods and fields,
or when blossoms that open with a welcoming to Spring
seem like a comforting caress
from them whose presence always will remain;
then peace and love will gain passage to your mind again,
and hold your heart in their embrace.

4/1984

Sunset in Falmouth (Photo by M. White, 10/13/2017)

Davis and Alexa and Me

Yesterday, I was sad, I was tired,
I was tired of being sad.

Glancing down, I saw his emerald eyes watching me.
"Ah," said I to my feline familiar,
"shall I ask Alexa to play our favorite song?"

He arose and brushed against my leg with his silky coat
and feather tail, which almost always means,
"Yes."

"Alexa, play *The Glory of Love*," which she did,
and I danced and I sang.

Davis joined in, first watching, then purring loudly,
then approving by slowly blinking his eyes.

"Yes," I answered, "you helped me chase the sadness away."

Sir Davis
Photo by Karen Ruggiero)

In the Garden

Frances greeted me with the most beautiful smile I'd ever seen.
Her smile lit up the room, AND my heart, the day we met.
We talked and learned a bit about each other;
she wanted to be able to walk on her own again
and then go home.
At each visit, we talked; she'd talk about going home,
but after a while, I knew that she knew, that was not to be.
So, once a week, our visits were filled with reminiscences
and songs.
With the songs, came more memories
of her family and friends.
Oh, how she loved her children and grandchildren, and the ones to come.
It took a while to grasp her sense of humor, for in addition to her ready smile and laugh,
she had a way to hide what she was thinking,
by closing her eyes.
I'd think she was drifting off to sleep-----but, no, just thinking,
perhaps of a question I had asked, or of a new thought laced
with joy and a funny memory.
Her smile was radiant with impish pleasure as she opened her eyes
and another story emerged.
She kept me on my toes, for her memory was better than mine.
A week or so before Elias was born, she said:
"I'm getting a new man in my life!".
Flabbergasted, I gawked. Frances continued------unperturbed at my confusion,
probably enjoying the look on my face---
and went on to predict the birth date of Elias.
As I walked in her door a week later, she called out:
"See, I was right, only a day off or so".
Yikes, just out of the blue--she had been awaiting my weekly entry,
and sooo enjoyed my "WHAT"? and flustered look.
We spent that time pouring over baby pictures and sharing more family
memories.
But near the end of our time together, she settled down and said:
"Could you write the words of your mother's favorite song for me?"
(I'd sung it several times during our visits and
over time, she'd sing along, sometimes closing her eyes.)
I wrote out all the verses that day, each followed by the chorus.
She studied it for a long time, and we sang it several times together,
ending with, "and the joys we shared as we tarried there,
none other has ever known."

Frances lives on in my heart.
I wish to thank Frances' entire family for their kindness in all approving this poem to be in *Spirit's Spark*.
After asking them and getting their enthusiastic permission, I understood even more about Frances.
Beautiful Lady, Beautiful Family.

Photo by Jan Butler
Opposite: Photo of Jan Butler by M. White

Re-Tuned Heart

After she left us, I could smile but not feel,
I could laugh, I could sing, but without any joy.
My soul just felt empty, just moldering on,
til I found the answer deep down in my heart.

My heart had to break before it could heal.
My heart was returned, when my heart was re-tuned,
letting love flood back once more
letting joy flood back once more.

The poems followed after, just one at a time,
The words flowed inside me, I didn't know why.
It's called an awakening, to me it's pure love
that was hiding deep down in my heart.

So, now when I sing, her sweet voice sings along;
And now when I dance, delight fills my soul.
From spiraling stars came the music again
that had hidden deep down in my heart.

My heart had to break before it could heal,
My heart was returned, when my heart was re-tuned,
letting love flood back once more
letting joy flood back once more.

This was written to be lyrics to a song, and it was,
but I wanted it in the book
as a tribute to my sister and as a tribute to a friend.

Skylands vista (Photo by Ruth Wilnor White)

Concerto

Beside the Salt Pond near the coast, sea grasses sighed
and swayed into the wind,
as Mendelssohn's concerto violin was weeping,
or just sounded that way.

Perhaps a violin can bring back times, as bow caresses strings,
so like the gentle brush of hand
upon a lover's cheek;
or melodies that soar and dip their wings into the sea,
as Osprey did today.

From years before, she'd kept the music deep within her heart,
the memories of the two of them
just holding hands,
allowing Mendelssohn to comfort them
yet for a little while.

And so, today, she listened to its haunting sounds,
and in her mind as they held hands,
the music played and sea grass danced
and brought them back together once again
for yet a little while.

Provincetown dunes (Photo by M. White)

Friendship

When friendship is a sacred thing
would it matter where we met,
if we met a thousand years ago
in the mountains of Tibet?
Or the Island of Tahiti
circled by an ocean blue,
where we listened to each other's words
and began a friendship true?
Ah, but it wasn't in Tahiti
or on Himalayan heights,
Even London or a Paris bus,
sharing stories in the night.
In a market
a tiny meeting hall
just you and I
the only ones at all.

Sometimes sitting on a park side bench,
people smiling, walking by
Somehow we knew above it all
we did not need to try.
For our Friendship forged itself before,
with Spirit's gift of grace
and sharing all our news and joys,
would set it's timely pace.

So here we are as years they go
still learning each new day,
as treasures grow
within our hearts,
somehow we find our way.

*This was one of 2 poems meant
to become a song, and so it has.*

Spirit's Spark

Photo by M. White

To Spirit

You taught me how to fly

I learned much more than could be
imagined;

that my soul could soar forever
in its weightlessness,
then, once again, to dance upon the Earth
in joyous return,

to sing when you would take me
up to Eagles' heights,

or to sleeping souls, who then
awaken to their memories found.

To Spirit in all your myriad, perfect forms,
my poems and songs begin and end
with gratitude.

You taught me how to fly

Goats and horses photos, both by Karen Ruggiero

A Question Poem and Its Answer

Question Poem from Milly to Karen
(after getting photo below, 4 pm)

Wow-Are they bringing in the slabs of stone
for the bottom of your steps?
Will they pull us to Stir Crazy at the end
of your busy day?
May we feed them chunks of carrots
when they carry us back home?
May I press my forehead to theirs
as I breathe into their noses?
Oh, beautiful draft horses, wish I were
back in time, when the day began
at 5 am, and sunset was its end.
I'd wash you and brush you and towel you all dry,
and wrap my arms around your neck,
and sing you words of praise.

Letter Poem back from Karen to Milly
(Karen was at Barnstable County Fair, 4:15pm

This just stopped me in my tracks.
Amid the noise and flashing lights
I had to read and continue reading
Laughing out loud.

Night Visitor

I first met him whilst he was in a cage.
Do not worry, for he was not trapped in one;
his bright, huge eyes showed no fear
as I stepped ever closer to him.
Eyes black and shining with an innocence
I had not seen when he'd flashed like a lightning bolt
from tree to tree
and edged his way with one last leap
toward the tube of seed.

The tube was surrounded by a "cage" to keep out squirrels.
Aha, the makers of this device had never seen a
flying squirrel navigate the tiny square holes.
Nor had I, until his brown and amber body
had found, at last, the sunflower seeds galore.
With little hands he gently took them from the tube
and saved some in his cheek for later on.

Marveling at his bravery, I moved yet closer still.
His coat appeared as silken fur which gathered
in a wrinkled cloak around his waist.
He thought to leave a few times, but stayed to gather more.
Then with evening meal complete, out he smoothly passed
through bars of steel
and flung himself through air and space.

Whilst reaching out with tiny hands and feet,
and stretching out his wrinkled cloak,
he made himself into a furry kite.
Flat rudder tail helped change his course
as I whispered a "Goodbye."
Somehow I knew we'd meet again,
as he sailed and leapt and sailed and leapt
and glided into night.

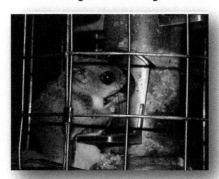

Photo by M. White

Celtic Music and the Fog

The green leaves of Oak, darkly glowing
in the noon time sun,
appeared as dusted with a coat of soft grey snow
in the evening fog.
Strange, this was the first time I'd noticed that effect on trees,
whilst returning home along Nantucket Sound.

"Ah," said I, as Celtic songs stirred memories
from many years before,
perceived in dreams, or stories read
about the Mists of Avalon.
Such a fog had hidden mystic lands that fed my thoughts
of long gone place and time.
Now, slow moving hooded persons,
faces shrouded by their capes,
became the Druid Elders planning ceremonies
upon the hazy Gaelic shores.
The deepening fog, combined with lilting music,
built this picture from afar.

Rapt with total contemplation, I did not know
who'd sent this gift of welcomed reminiscence.
One thing I know for sure about this stirring mystery,
I must thank the ancient Celtic music
and my velvet island fog.

Grasmere Pond (Photo by M. White)

The Messenger

She soared above us, catching upper currents
while her broad dark wings were still.
Focusing at first her hooded golden eyes on Mount Defiance,
she turned her great white head toward Grasmere's valley far below.
A snowy cloud was low enough to screen her moving shadow,
in a slow and spiraling flight.
Unafraid, the horses only added to this dream-like scene
with their quiet munching of the soft sweet hay.
Back then, I did not know that Eagle was a messenger,
this visit was her first.

A spirit guide, she forecast the awakenings,
not remembered from the times before,
and left behind in childhood days.
Left behind with "knowing", as the years just went along.
Yet close she stayed, and deep inside I felt the tidings that she'd brought;
many which I would not see, and many that I could not hear.

Then from early Spring to late December and beyond,
the messages were carried on her fluttering wings;
and I was told to grasp the golden cords of promises
from many stars far past the Milky Way.
And thus they filled my dreams,
and thus they filled my heart.
Until I knew and felt the Spirit's call,
carried in by Eagle's wings at last.

Martha's Vineyard (Photo-by M. White)

Last Night

Last night you were in a dream,
more of an answered prayer than dream,
for you had turned your head to me
as you were moving forward,
your face radiating renewed faith, and energy
and joy.
I knew, I knew that your smile was one with Spirit's,
as was the answered prayer for Grace.

Provincetown dunes (Photo-by M. White)

Winter robins (Photo by M. White)

Echoes

Spirit echoes from my poems, for Spirit is in each of us,

calling from the core of our existence,

two footed or four, winged or bound to Earth,

or rising from the ocean depths in harmony

with waves and wind.

And yes, the mighty Oak that's standing steady in a storm,

the sea grass bending gracefully in dance,

and flowers drawing in the butterflies and bees.

All our calls will echo from and through the greatest heights

or from the lowest plains,

until that time of recognition in and of each other,

when we see, and we know,

the Divine.

Photo by M. White

Afterthoughts

Colonial Theater

Oh, my,
It seems a place left far behind
in the golden age of theater;
when ladies, with their hair in lace,
with their dresses skirting the marble floors,
sat in high, gold, fashion box seats,
with fans before their faces,
eagerly awaiting the curtain's rising
and the start of the orchestra below.
Silence, then applause,
as the handsome Tenor, in his black tuxedo,
began the Aria,
which made the ladies blush with joy.

Photo by T. Arthur

Sand Dollars and Dolphins

Once again, my memories shift to younger years,
magical, mysterious years, years of overwhelming joy
and perhaps a bit of sadness just thrown in
to even things out in a teenager's life.
Poems of mine reflect those memories sometimes
when they are gifts from the Milky Way
or beyond. (I still believe some are.)
But today the gift of memory was enclosed
in a lovely perfect sand dollar at a vendor's booth,
hung on a ribbon of silken white.
For when I saw it, instantly the past returned.

I saw again the sleek grey bodies
pass me by,
as they arched and dove, arched and dove
back into the Florida sea.
Bright black eyes of the entire family pod
locked on mine as they continued on,
not but a few feet away.
My searching for sand dollars on a narrow sand bank
----that then dropped off into the ocean depths-----
had brought these Dolphins near enough
for me to touch, for me to call out to,
for me to follow.
It was as in a dream, my leaden feet
and awkward body trapped me, and I could not move,
my soul quite ready to swim free, to join the pod,
their eyes welcoming and unafraid.

The gift today, three score years later,
let me dive into the green-blue sea at last,
grasp a dorsal fin
and join my comrades for at least a while,
for this ride of a lifetime.

Poems Returned

So, in the CD section I stood
and searched and searched
for Kedrov's *Our Father*.
Perhaps you already have that beautiful
recording,
but perhaps not;
so I kept up the search and found an Enya
and a Carly Simon, I'd not
heard before.

THEN, (and, no, not Kedrov
not even a CD),
but books in the next row,
one was of poetry.

I held my tears until in the car,
opened Mary Oliver's *Dog Songs*,
read several
and let the tears gently flow.
Interesting how some things happen.
Interesting how poems begin again, when
they have waited in a muted soul.

12/8/18

About the Author

Milly White was a Public Health, Terminal Oncology, Hospice, and Visiting Nurse for many years in New Jersey, as well as on Cape Cod. She also boarded horses, had lots of wonderful animals who got along with each other and a parrot named Laura, at a beautiful, mystical place named Grasmere, in New Jersey. As mentioned in the Introduction, she suddenly became and now identifies herself as a poet. Poetry is her communication of choice.